BEINN EIGHE

Britain's First National Nature Reserve

ISBN 1 85397 177 4
A CIP record is held at the British Library.

PHOTOGRAPHY BY:

Niall Benvie: Back Cover, 11, 13, 17, 20, 22, 23, 48, 50, 51, 54TL, 54BR, 83, 88TL, 88BL, 88R, 89, 95

Laurie Campbell: Front Cover A, B & D, 35, 36, 37, 38, 39, 41TL, 41TR, 41BL, 45, 49, 52, 53, 54TR, 54BL, 55, 56, 58, 59, 60, 61, 62, 66, 68, 79, 80, 81, 82, 86

Lorne Gill: Front Cover, 10, 15, 18, 25, 32, 33, 34

John MacPherson: 1, 3, 4, 6, 8, 9, 12, 14, 16, 19, 21, 26, 27, 28, 29, 30, 31 40, 42, 43, 44, 46, 47, 57, 63, 64, 65, 67, 69, 70, 71, 72, 73, 74, 75, 76, 77, 78, 84, 85, 87, 90, 91, 92, 93L, 93TR, 93BR, 94

David Whitaker: Front Cover C, 7, 24, 41BR

AUTHOR: Kenny Taylor / SNH

MAP: Wendy Price

DESIGN AND PRODUCTION: Colin Baxter Photography Ltd

FRONT COVER PHOTOGRAPH: *An Sgurra Bàn and Na Bodaich Dhubha (Black Carls), Beinn Eighe*
BACK COVER PHOTOGRAPH: *Liaghach and Beinn Eighe from Loch Clàr*
PAGE 1 PHOTOGRAPH: *Quartzite screes, Beinn Eighe*
PAGE 3 PHOTOGRAPH: *Silhouetted pines, Loch Clàr*

Scottish Natural Heritage
Anancaun
Kinlochewe
By Achnasheen
Ross-shire
IV22 2PD
Tel: 01445-760254
Fax: 01445-760301
E-mail: pubs@redgore.demon.co.uk
Web site http://www.snh.org.uk

Printed in China

BEINN EIGHE

Britain's First National Nature Reserve

This publication presents a memorable fusion of pictures and words focusing on Beinn Eighe National Nature Reserve. Scottish Natural Heritage commissioned some of Scotland's leading photographers and a prominent environmental author to visit and capture the spirit of this unique place through the seasons. The result is this elegant portrait of the reserve and its surroundings.

With the exception of a few wildlife images, all the photographs were taken on and around Beinn Eighe. The landscape photography includes views of areas outwith the reserve, but these images serve to set Beinn Eighe in its wider context. This evocative profile represents a fitting celebration of the grandeur and appeal of this much-loved Highland asset.

Beinn Eighe from Coulin

CONTENTS

Introduction

Relic pinewood in the Allt an Doire Dharaich gorge *(left)*

Pine marten *(right)*

Tansley Bog

Even in the centre of Kinlochewe village you can feel it. Not just the mountain flank that shoulders down towards the houses, or the clouds that can swirl like giant's breath just beyond the edge of the village. Not just the green and brown of old pines on the near slopes as you head west along Loch Maree, or the sound of a stag's bellow echoing from the crags as you take the Torridon road.

No, it's not just one of these things, but all of them. And countless more besides, bringing a sense of wildness close, tantalising with proximity, yet challenging with scale. Whether in a major hike through the hills, a short amble in the woods or just pausing to look and appreciate the scene, Beinn Eighe has a presence that can't be ignored. For some, it's a pleasant part of a longer journey; for others, it's the backdrop to their daily business; for a few, it's a lifetime of study.

So it seems particularly fitting that this place, which brings wildness within reach of many, yet holds within its landscapes a complexity not easily defined, should have been singled out as the first National Nature Reserve (NNR) in Britain. The declaration was

Beinn an Eòin and An t-Sàil Mhòr

made in November, 1951: 'The Nature Conservancy has purchased by private treaty a property in the County of Ross and Cromarty. It will be known as Beinn Eighe Nature Reserve.'

'The woodlands include both birch and pine,' it continued. 'The animal life is varied; pine martens, wild cats, deer and foxes are to be seen. Among the birds observed in the area are golden eagle, buzzard, merlin and many species of smaller birds... The reserve as a whole offers excellent opportunities for ecological study.'

Half a century later and many other accolades have followed, recognising both the national and international significance of Beinn Eighe's wildlife and landscape, as well as the enormous scope to learn from the particular combinations of circumstances here.

Rock strata whose arrangement and fossils give evidence of continent-shaping events over hundreds of millions of years; native woods whose ancestry holds an unbroken link back to trees that came here not long after the Ice Age; communities of plants whose abundance and health depend on moist, Atlantic-driven weather over centuries and decades; the dragonfly whose

Common polypody fern amongst woodland mosses

Coille na Glas-leitir woodland (opposite)

emergence from a bog pool means the sun on that particular morning has warmed the water to an ideal temperature – these are some of the timescales and strands of life that can be brought together at Beinn Eighe.

Some 4800 hectares are within the NNR now, stretching southwest from Loch Maree and Kinlochewe to the dark cleft of An Coire Dubh Mòr that divides the Beinn Eighe range from Liaghach. Within this sit huge sweeps of ridge and slope, set in a wider landscape of other mountains, lochs and glens.

Liaghach

There are many ways of describing the richness that is held here. A botanist might speak of the alpine heaths and dry heaths that hold an unusual variety and abundance of mosses and other small plants. A geneticist would ponder the ancestral links between the Scots pines at Beinn Eighe and those in the pinewoods of Spain and southern France. Those with an eye for birds and mammals might think first about birds of prey, divers and martens and the wild cats that so often stalk unseen.

A climber's mind would immediately turn to the sandstone and quartzite layers of the Triple Buttress, and to strange sounding route names like 'Boggle' and 'Birth of the Cool'. Artists and photographers would visualise a wealth of views and angles, with the shifting light under fast-changing clouds giving scope for fresh interpretation and inspiration.

One place, many responses, countless possibilities. Huge as a mountain range, tiny as a midge bite. Distant as a fossil trace, close as the coolness of raindrops on skin. Loud as a hill burn in spate, quiet as a gliding eagle.

Stone, water, air, earth and spirit in many forms: behold Beinn Eighe.

Triple Buttress in Coire Mhic Fhearchair
and An t-Sàil Mhòr

Beinn Eighe from Coulin

Liaghach from Beinn Eighe (opposite)

Stone

Spiodan Coire nan Clach and An Sgurra Bàn from Liaghach (left)

Quartzite (right)

Mention Beinn Eighe to someone who knows Scottish mountains and they're sure to talk about rock. That might seem obvious, since all mountains are constructs of stone. But not all have the beauty and strangeness of stone that sets Beinn Eighe apart.

From above Glen Torridon to the south, or gliding as an eagle might do, over the isolated mass of Meall a' Ghiuthais to the north, the ridges of the massif seem to radiate from the point called Spiodan Coire nan Clach, *pinnacle of the corrie of stones*. The main rocky spine to the east and west of it is narrow, with challenging sections towards the extreme ends.

But at any point along these routes, you need a sureness of step and a grasp of timing and tactics. Tarry too long as the clouds pile in, miscalculate the hours needed to return down and along a glen, and the warmth of Kinlochewe at the mountain skirts can suddenly seem remote and hard to gain.

Weathered sandstone by Loch Maree

Looking north from Beinn Eighe ridge (opposite)

That can be the way of it with mountains: an edginess around the exhilaration of being tested by steep slopes and dizzying drops, the adrenalin charge that gives extra clarity to perception of details.

The view across scree slopes and boglands to loch, sea and other mountains; the middle ground where a burn draws an exquisite calligraphy of channel line; the boulder and its coarseness under boot or hand – these are things that can etch in the mind for years when gained in a place where your own position is not assured. Strange, then, that a sense of calm can come from such apparent insecurity, with a warmth of memory that glows in recollection of the challenge tackled.

Beinn Eighe, like many mountains, can be like that for some who seek its upper limits. But it also figures strongly in the perception of many who would not choose to clamber its core. For you can't ignore the look of it.

Summit of the main ridge is An Sgurra Bàn, *the white peak*. At

Fragmented quartzite

972 metres, it falls just short of the top of the whole massif at An Ruadh-stac Mòr, *the greater red steep hill*. But the visual impact of *the white peak* and its outriders can be enormous.

Beneath the ridges, the mountain flanks are streaked and dappled with huge swatches of white and grey. In strong sunlight, the effect can be dazzling. In overcast, the brightness still sings, as if lit by some strange power source from the heart of the mountain. Like snowfields in high summer – as many folk have

Common violet,
Meall a' Ghiuthais

commented – they present Beinn Eighe with a look that is utterly different from the leviathan of Liaghach to the south, or the looming bulk of Slioch to the north.

In one way, there's no mystery to the source of bright beauty. It comes from quartzite, a stone made almost entirely of the mineral quartz. This is a crystalline form of silica – one of the most abundant minerals in the Earth's crust and the major ingredient in sand.

More than 500 million years ago, the 'basal' quartzite at Beinn

Eighe (a hard, pale rock that can look a bit like Kendal mint cake) was sand. That much seems straightforward, although the geological forces needed to compress and change sand grains to slabs of hard, white rock can seem hard to comprehend. But things get even more challenging, stretching limits of imagination and understanding as the screes and summits stretch stamina and willpower.

Fir clubmoss

Go to the extreme – to the age of the Lewisian gneiss that is the bedrock, hidden by later sediments in much of Torridon – and the span of some three billion years since its moulding seems beyond those mental limits. Reel-in, and the 800 to 1000 million year vintage of Torridonian sandstones (formed in the outwash of rivers at the fringe of a vanished continent and piled several kilometres deep over the old Lewisian plain) still seems out of reach.

But the time of the sediments that would lead to the quartzite, though distant, is less strange. This Cambrian period, beginning 570 million years ago, was when a glorious diversity of higher life-forms burst onto the global scene. Not bacterial pinpricks and algal blobs, but creatures that crawled, wriggled, waved tentacles, swam.

The imprint of some of them is still here, stippled across stone surfaces like lumpy porridge, showing as straight lines in sections of shattered boulder. 'Pipe rock' is the name for these fossil-bearing rocks, their marks formed from the burrows of tube-dwelling worms that fed in the shallows of an ocean long gone, by a continent so altered and re-fashioned by later planet scrapings

Beinn Eighe ridge from
An Coire Dubh Mòr

that its name *Laurentia* seems more of sci-fi than of Earth.

In a few places here, other traces of Cambrian marine life are held in stone, their presence giving pointers to how the continents were once arranged. Primitive sea-urchin-like creatures are among these fossils. So too are trilobites: hard-shelled, bug-eyed, distant relatives of insects, crabs and spiders.

Ptarmigan in summer plumage

Na Bodaich Dhubha (Black Carls)
on Sgùrr nam Fear Dubha
(opposite)

Some of the trilobites at Beinn Eighe are similar to ones that lived in what is now Canada and Greenland at the same time. They're different though from those in England and Scandinavia – evidence of a time in the planet's history when Scotland and England lay an ocean apart.

Hard to grasp, certainly. But like the touch of fingers on the surface of a pipe rock boulder, the stones of Beinn Eighe can put this kind of challenge within reach.

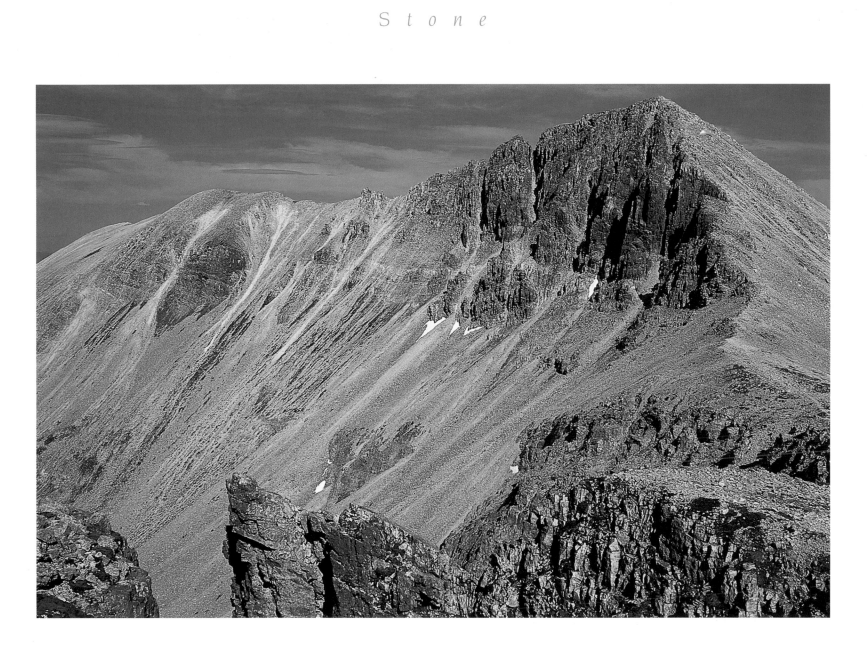

Sgùrr nam Fear Dubha

An Ruadh-stac Beag from An Sgurra Bàn (opposite)

Looking west from Na Bodaich Dhubha (Black Carls)

Quartzite textures, An Sgurra Bàn (opposite)

An Ruadh-stac Mòr from An Sgurra Bàn

An Sgurra Bàn from Coire nan Laogh

Na Bodaich Dhubha (Black Carls)

Liaghach (opposite)

Air

Early morning cloud between Beinn Eighe and Liaghach (left)

Cottongrass (right)

Breathe in deeply and you can inhale some of the essence of this place. Out on the moor, the scent of bog myrtle – warming, aromatic and fresh – in counterpoint to the denser tones of moss and peat. Within the wood, the tang of pine resin, the sweet mouldering of fallen branches and the nutty aroma of fungi.

Among the old pines, the early morning air is still. No swaying of branches, no shiver of twig or stem in ling and bracken below. Yet it swirls with sounds, pushes evidence of unseen lives and hidden movements forward, like ripples moving through its invisible medium.

Young golden eagle over Beinn Eighe

Somewhere above the trees, a buzzard is calling as it soars higher, riding a thermal of the warming day. Closer, a hiss of water snakes along a channel where a burn has cut its course over thousands of years, constantly refreshing its connection between mountain source and loch basin.

Above the burn sound, a willow warbler sends a sweet, high

tumble of notes to cascade from a birch tree. It pauses, as if to emphasize the skill of this sudden, jazzy flourish. Then it sings again, staking claim to this part of the wood, this portion of morning.

There are fainter sounds too: the crack of a pine cone prised apart by a crossbill; a whirr of wings above the path that winds uphill through the trees. Whirr ends in click, as a dragonfly lands on a sunlit boulder. It's a large one, with several centimetres of black body hooped with yellow. A dozen other kinds of dragonfly have flown over high ground and low here during the months of summer.

Tawny owlet in Grudie pinewood

Three of these are scarce in Scotland. Rarest of all is the gloriously named 'northern emerald'. The dark green glint of it still shines over boggy pools among the heathland and near trees on the mountain flanks. This is one of the few places in the Highlands where it survives and these Scottish refuges are all that remain for its species in Britain.

Its larvae live in shallow water and among bog mosses. So they're fiendishly difficult to find and to study by those with an eye for 'Odonata', as this ancient group of insects is known. But a handful of people with a passion for them keeps trying, summer after summer, to pluck some measurements from the ooze and better understand these gems of the bog pools.

Creeping lady's-tresses

The white-faced darter and the azure hawker (a sun seeker that shelters among heather and moor grasses in dull weather) complete the trio of scarce peat-pool dragons. The basker on the boulder is none of these. Golden-ringed is its name – a fitting title to crown its status as the longest-bodied of all the myriad insects that live at Beinn Eighe.

Not for it the calm of bog pools. The female seeks flowing water in burns and runnels, pokes her several-centimetre-long abdomen beneath the surface and sticks eggs to the grit of the stream bed. For several years, the hatched larvae remain there.

Then they change shape and shift elements, sloughing larval skin, emerging from water and unfurling four translucent wings. For a few weeks they ride the breeze and are boosted by sunlight:

creatures of air with a mastery of flight fine-tuned by their kind since before the time of dinosaurs.

Farther uphill, the air is cooler, with a noticeable chilling in every few score metres of ascent. Whatever the weather, from up here the sky seems huge and close. Whether a dome of blue, a wash of grey or a canopy of burnished reds and golds, streaked with high clouds at sunset, there's no ignoring its presence.

Seen against this vastness, even the silhouette of an eagle, broad-winged and blunt-tailed, can seem like a speck against sky and skyline. Only the mountains themselves are equal to the backdrop, although even they can be dwarfed by the piles of storm clouds pushed against them by winds from the sea.

When a gale stills, the view clears and the day draws breath, Beinn Eighe can seem charged with wonder. Scent of moor, sound of wood song, whirr of insect wings, carried on the warming air that cloaks the mountain.

Cross-leaved heath

Beinn Eighe from above Loch Clàr

White-faced darter dragonfly

Northern emerald dragonfly

Azure hawker dragonfly

Emerald damselfy

Beinn Eighe from Glen Grudie

Looking west from Coire Mhic Fhearchair

Liaghach from Glen Torridon

Wind sculpted pine

Wind-blown birch woodland,
Glen Bianasdail

Beinn Eighe ridge
from Liaghach (opposite)

Earth

Lichens *(left)*

Green tiger beetle *(right)*

Cloudberry

Beinn Eighe isn't blessed with soil you could call rich. The rocks and the weather combine to limit the possibilities. No dark loams here, or fertile red earths like those in the eastern lowlands. The quartzite and sandstone that make up most of the surface stones are poor in plant boosting chemicals. Occasional exceptions to this happen where water percolates over other rocks, such as mudstone (that difference is reflected in grassy flushes, studded with alpine lady's-mantle and other herbs). But acidity and coolness are the more general rule.

Up among the boulders along summit plateaux and in the screes that fan down steep slopes, little soil can form. Conditions are unstable here, with snow melt, rock slide and slope creep all adding to the difficulty for plants to keep hold, spread and, through their dying and recycling by fungi, insects and microscopic creatures, help to build up any substantial cloaking of soil.

The lichens, too, make what they can of tough conditions, clamped so low on stones that they can look like paint splashes. They would have been among the first major lifeforms to move back here, after the land had been scraped clean by the Ice Age glaciers. A blank slate, then spores blew in and settled in the tiniest of crevices, followed by lichen colour providing one of the first signs, small but bold, that a new life chapter had begun.

It took another 2000 years, perhaps, before the first Scots pines could take root on the low ground, some 8250 years ago. Their ancestral stock may have weathered the big freeze somewhere out to the west where conditions were just mild enough for survival. These northwest mainland trees are still a little different from Scots pine in the central Highlands, their uniqueness revealed in their chemical make-up.

Crowberry

Conditions were excellent for pine growth for another two millennia beyond their return, after which cooler, wetter weather began to prevail. This cramped the possibilities for Scots pines in the northwest and boosted the boglands. The rain-fed blankets of *Sphagnum* mosses swelled and spread, cloaking low ground and hollows, restricting trees.

But in places where slopes and well-drained soils allowed, Scots pines and the other native trees that grew in their company could hold their ground. In times to come, many parts of the old forest would dwindle and vanish, as pressures from grazing animals, fire and felling took their toll. But the pinewoods at Beinn Eighe weathered all changes, including a blaze that swept through in the 1700s, leaving a layer of charcoal in the woodland soil today that remains to mark its passage. Though much reduced in size and altered in character, they survived. Through them, an unbroken link remains to trees that returned in the wake of the ice.

Common lizard by the
Allt an Doire Dharaich gorge

That bond makes a wealth of other life possible here, from branch to trunk, root and soil, including the survival of many kinds of small invertebrates — creatures without backbones — such as insects and spiders. Dead or alive, the trees feed and shelter whole communities of them.

Some of these wee beasties are tiny, like those whose larvae can live within Scots pine needles, or only in damp pine rot holes.

Others are eyecatchers, like the timberman beetle, the male of which has antennae longer than his body. The web of their relationships has hardly begun to be untangled through study. What is certain is that they play a complex part in the flow and recycling of materials from tree to soil and back again within the woods, as different communities also do in the grasslands, heaths and other places where life has flourished here.

Under bark, inside cones, needles and leaves, among dead wood, leaf litter and fungi sit opportunities for insects and others to find their niche. Under frost-shattered boulders, among wet moss, in thin soil and in the water of bog pools are some of the life spaces beyond the trees.

Sawflies, hoverflies, gnats, weevils and moths are some of the insects that can grab such opportunities. And beetles, the roll-call of whose group names has a poetry of its own, each entry pointing to a band of many species. Rove, cardinal, leaf and longhorn; darkling, ambrosia and ground. Creatures of the crevices, the chambers and hollows. From tree root to mountain top, salt of this earth.

Pinewood fungus

Woodland mosses

Moorland liverwort

Sphagnum bog mosses

Ostrich plume moss

Scotch argus butterfly

Red deer stag

Loch Maree from the head of Glen Docherty (opposite)

Patterns in pine, Pony Path

Pine skeleton, Coille na Glas-leitir (opposite)

Emperor moth caterpillar

Scots pine seedling (opposite)

Common toad by Loch Maree

Moss carpeted pine

Water

Abhainn an Easaigh, Glen Bianasdail (left)

Winter spate (right)

They swept in from the west in April, these spirits of the loch, while snow clung to high ridges and icicles gleamed like winter teeth at the edge of hill cascades. Through the mist that hangs in morning chill come their cries: wailing, rising, fading and swelling in waves of sound, echoing through woods and from rocks by the shore.

*Loch Maree from
Glen Grudie*

**Black-throated diver
on Loch Maree** (opposite)

Black-throated divers: the name seems almost too matter-of-fact to catch the essence of these creatures of air and water. Part of one of the most ancient winged groups, their looks show how close the fit now is between bird and liquid. It's not so much the neck blackness, but the streaks, patches and flecks of white over chest and back. The natural artistry of ripples, dappled shallows and shimmering droplets is written there; the glint of fish scales and the dark of unseen deeps.

Some think such feather patterns could have a practical purpose, with the wavy lines and speckles helping to break up the bird's outline underwater. This could help it chase fish, and give camouflage against aerial predators or would-be nest attackers. Whatever the reason, theirs is a primal beauty, and rare indeed, with the black-throat clan now dwindled to a few score pairs in Scotland.

Palmate newt by Pony Path

Water is the setting, the support and the shaping for so much at Beinn Eighe. Loch Maree draws the eye along the northern flank, its flat expanse holding brightness from sky and reflections from slopes – an opposite to the scene all around. In calm you could see trees and crags and flying birds all mirrored there, but held in two dimensions, a world away from the infinite lumps and folds of the scene beyond the water.

Away from the big loch, the mountains, heaths and woods are still framed and energised by water. The burn that roils and tumbles through a glen, the fall that spills for tens of metres down a sharp-cut face, the lochan that sits beneath soaring buttresses, the bog pools catching sun glints far out on the sodden plain: these are not mere add-ons to the rocky heart of this place. They are part of its pulse, what makes it come to life.

Walk the glen and hear the burn, touch the splash of waterfall, see the rock walls caught in the lochan glass, feel the seep of bog water under boot, the clamminess of rain through clothing. Then you'll know some of the power of water here.

But there's so much more. Like the way the very look of the ground is a legacy of frozen water. Ice by the glacier load, swelled hundreds of metres high. Ice that carved the bowl curves of corries, plucked rocks from headwalls to shape cliffs, severed burn courses from their smooth, slow descents to spawn waterfalls. Ice on the move, trenching glen sides, channelling hollows for loch and lochan, spreading gravel, dumping boulders.

White water-lilies
on Loch Coulin

And for 10,000 years and more, water has continued to work the surfaces fashioned in those glacial mills of the Ice Age. More slowly, much more slowly, but relentless. Drip and flow, freeze and thaw, the invisible working of water-borne chemicals on stone, all fed by the copious rains.

It can rain here on nearly two days out of three in an average year, with plenty of cloud cover on the usual day. The nearness of the sea, and the breath of westerlies, warmed by Atlantic currents, delivers the soaking and doesn't stint on the quantity.

From that outpouring, whether as rain or as damp cloud that

transfers moisture to plants by clinging in droplets on their surfaces, comes part of Beinn Eighe's natural bounty. Plants that thrive in cool,

Beinn Eighe from Loch Clàr

Loch Coulin (opposite)

wet conditions love it here. Mosses and liverworts – small plants that lack roots and so take their moisture straight, through drips and mist-borne vapour – do particularly well. So do lichens that like moist 'oceanic' conditions and ferns that thrive in cool, dank shade.

Some of the mosses and liverworts are found in few other places in the world, yet they revel in Beinn Eighe's cool, damp climate. These include a large, patch-forming moss *(Dicranum subporodictyon)* whose only known locations are here, British Columbia and western China.

Even rarer is a large, orange-brown liverwort *(Herbertus borealis)* for which Beinn Eighe is the world headquarters (its only other bases are a handful of sites in Norway). Quite why this choosy, moisture-loving rarity has taken to this part of Torridon in such a big way is a bit of a mystery. But like the divers, their patterns and their haunting cries, there's still much to be fathomed in the waters of Beinn Eighe.

Autumn colour, Loch Clàr

Loch Maree and Slioch

View west from Coire Mhic Fhearchair

Glen Bianasdail (opposite)

Liaghach from Loch Clàr

Loch Maree from Coille na Glas-leitir (opposite)

Spirit

Glen Torridon (left)

Golden eagle (right)

Mountain azalea

How do you get your bearings in such a landscape of mountain and woodland, bog and loch? What do you need, both to navigate and to know this place?

Some would say that it's easy in an age of high-tech aids. Just press a button on the hand-held global positioning system, send a signal to a satellite and watch the display reveal, to within a few metres, your geographical co-ordinates.

Compass and map could be helpful, too, the cartography fine-tuned with the aid of aerial photographs and images from space to show the ground plan and elevation, helping you move from this point to that. But what of those who came before with few or any such aids?

Did they stumble more from the lack of them, know less of the land and its life? Or did they move with sureness of foot through a landscape made alive by a different way of seeing it, and by a different sense of their own place and path within it?

There's no telling how it was for the first people who came this way. Wandering groups of hunter-gatherers could have moved through some of the earliest pinewood to grow here, not much more than two millennia after the Ice Age closed, but leaving no trace yet found. In the thousands of years beyond them there are almost no pointers to what later travellers or residents might have done hereabouts.

Only when Vikings came to raid and settle part of Ross-shire, a thousand and more years ago, do some human images start to materialise on the screen. But the focus is fuzzy, the details partly lost. Torridon names like Shieldaig, *herring bay,* and various 'dales' give snatches of Norse speech but there is little more to speak of, despite the importance of Viking settlement in Ross-shire.

In the Middle Ages and beyond, when the Clan Mackenzie held sway over much of the area, flashes of greater clarity come, in fragments of recorded history and in those Gaelic names that survived long enough to be still remembered in recent years. The 13th century may have generated the name Coire Mhic Fhearchair, *the corrie of the son of Farquhar.*

Prostrate juniper

This is the corrie that some hold to be the grandest in all Scotland, with its lochan reflecting the towering glory of the Triple Buttress. It seems a fitting place to honour the son of Farquhar Macintaggart, first Earl of Ross.

This time could also have been when Sgùrr nan Conbhair, *the peak of the dog-men*, would have recalled to local folk an incident in a deer hunt over the hills, making them look to the skyline and imagine people, scene and sounds in ways we can only guess at.

Then the butchery at the Kinlochewe River wrote its name in blood at Àth nan Ceann, *the ford of the heads*. Followers of Leod MacGilleandreis were decapitated by Black Murdo of the Cave and his band in a 14th-century feud, and their heads came ashore upstream of what has long been known as a good fishing pool.

Barred red moth

Less dramatic, but no less poignant, are the names that speak of natural features, some now gone: Toll a' Ghiuthais, *the hollow of the fir*, where no pine now grows; An Doire Daraich, *the oak hollow*, with no acorn, sapling or tree.

But others still strike such a chord that they sound through the ages to spark recognition and understanding in mind: Coir' an Anmoich, *the corrie of the gloaming,* for example, at the lower part of the pass that runs between the mountain masses of Liaghach and Beinn Eighe. It would often have been dusk when hunters returning from the hills reached the corrie foot, just as it can be near nightfall when walkers who have tarried on the Beinn Eighe tops get back to the car park close by here.

And with that recognition can come a sense both of loss and of possibilities. The folk that coined and used the Gaelic names are now fading in memory here – the crofters, herders, hunters,

Evening light on Grudie pinewood

stalkers, lairds and shepherds, blacksmiths, weavers and others. They could read this land not just as a set of co-ordinates, or a collection of categories.

The names they used made the place come alive, with people, events and descriptions of features – steep, flat, brown, yellow, quiet, windy and more – that lit hill and glen with meaning, and set human life within its beam. That kind of relationship with place may not readily come again here. But there are other opportunities.

For there are layers of meaning in the wider life of Beinn Eighe, the life other than human that people can nonetheless perceive, respect and nurture. The tree nursery workers that painstakingly gather pine cones for seeds, then plant them, tend them and take them out to help the old woods expand again – they know something with both mind and heart.

A rambler can know it after a good day on the hill, or a child who has just seen her first dragonfly close at hand. So too do the researchers that devote years of intellect and passion to this one, amazing portion of the globe. Like the scientist whose study has

View over Loch nan Cabar from Beinn Eighe

View west from Coire Mhic Fhearchair (opposite)

been the small junipers that prostrate themselves on wind-blasted ridges, whose gnarled stems are like symbols of life struggling against adversity.

Making her way along a remote part of the hill where they grow, the snow has drifted and hidden stone and stem. A blustering gale holds the temperature sub-zero, whirls a stinging spindrift of crystals.

The scientist pauses, removes her gloves and brushes some snow from a juniper. Twists of wood and the spiked greenery of foliage, sharp as the snow against bare hands, are revealed in slow, respectful moves.

Mountain hare

A' Chreag Dhubh (opposite)

She talks quietly about what being here at Beinn Eighe, with that plant, at that moment, in that snow on the mountain means. Then she smiles and falls quiet.

And there's a joy in that silence. Something beyond naming, beyond words.

Scots pine bark on moss

Moss on birch

Lichen on birch

Thyme and alpine lady's-mantle

Spiodan a' Choire Lèith, Liaghach *Glen Grudie* (opposite)

Looking over Kinlochewe to Beinn Eighe

Hillwalkers on A' Chreag Dhubh

Footpath team

Volunteer tree planting

Beinn Eighe from Coulin

Scots pine seedling

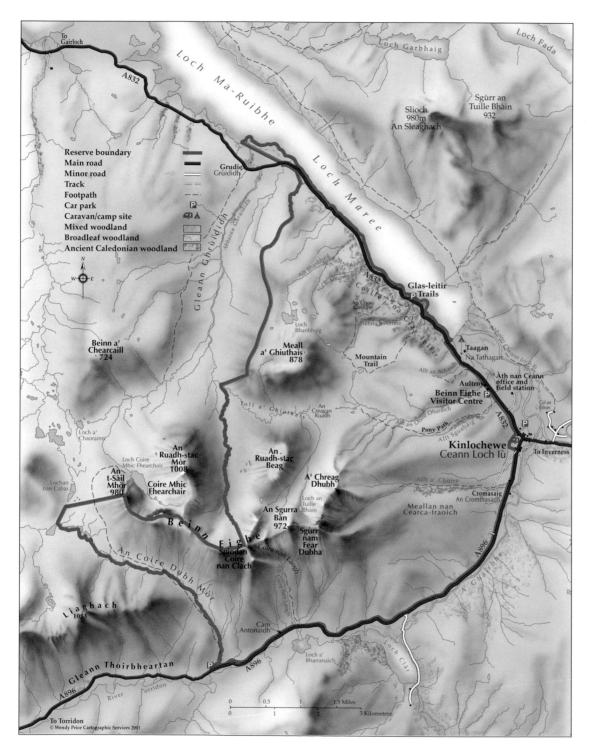

Beinn Eighe NNR lies at the southeast end of Loch Maree, near the village of Kinlochewe in Wester Ross. It can be accessed from both the A832 and A896 roads.

To help you get the most from your time on the reserve, there's an 'access for all' visitor centre just outside Kinlochewe, along with three associated low ground trails. The centre is open from spring to autumn and the trails are accessible throughout the year.

Other facilities for the public include the two self-guided Glas-leitir Woodland and Mountain Trails, which start beside the main A832 road. Trail guides are available for these wonderful walks, which take you through the heart of the ancient woodland or up onto the rugged mountain tops above Loch Maree.